# NICK

# SpongeBob SquarePants™

## THE ESSENTIAL GUIDE

Written by
David Lewman

SANDY CHEEKS

PLANKTON

PATRICK STAR

# NICK
# SpongeBob squarepants

## THE ESSENTIAL GUIDE

SPONGEBOB
SQUAREPANTS

**DK**

# Contents

# SpongeBob SquarePants

Absorbent, yellow, and porous, SpongeBob lives in a pineapple under the sea with his pet snail, Gary. He's an optimistic sponge, who's enthusiastic about everything he does. He loves to blow bubbles, flip Krabby Patties at the Krusty Krab, play with his friends, and make people laugh!

## Dressing up

In SpongeBob's closet hang neatly arranged, identical ensembles of his favorite clothing— white shirt, red tie, striped socks, black shoes, and square (of course) brown pants held up with a stylish black belt. While some might think otherwise, SpongeBob likes to think of himself as very fashionable.

*Holes keep SpongeBob buoyant and light on his feet!*

SpongeBob knows that the perfect Krabby Patty is made with love. SpongeBob is full of love—for his job, for his pet snail, for Bikini Bottom, for his friends, and even for himself! His heart is as true as his pants are square.

*SpongeBob can tear himself in half— and grow back together!*

# Bubble bliss

SpongeBob is so good at blowing bubbles, he's fully qualified to give lessons. For a nominal fee, which he'll gladly loan you, he'll be happy to show you his patented bubble-blowing technique. To SpongeBob, bubbles are more than mere spheres of soapy liquid. They're an art form, a means of communication, and the source of a friend, like Bubble Buddy.

## "I'm ready!"

*If SpongeBob's arms fall off he can just grow new ones!*

## Gritty customer

SpongeBob may face a lot of obstacles in his undersea existence, but he usually comes out a winner in the end. Whether it's a crowd of hungry anchovies or a band of pineapple-devouring nematodes, SpongeBob takes on all obstacles. He's full of grit, determination, and a fair amount of salt water.

Though he loves his work, SpongeBob also loves holidays, even if they're holidays you've never heard of, like Leif Ericsson Day or Opposite Day. He dives into celebrating with gusto.

## Sponge Facts

There are about 5,000 species of sponges in the sea world. Sponges can grow back body parts that fall off!

# Patrick Star

Patrick's life is complicated. Because he's a starfish, he loves to cling to his rock, sleep, and eat, but because he's SpongeBob's best friend, he participates in lots of exciting adventures away from home. He even went to the moon in Sandy's rocket!

## "I can't understand anything."

## A loyal star

Patrick is a very loyal and sensitive friend. The mere thought of SpongeBob moving away can make him weep, sob, and moan. Of course, the thought of missing breakfast can also make him weep, sob, and moan. Whenever you need Patrick, you can count on him being there for you—even if he's asleep.

*Patrick won an award for "Doing Absolutely Nothing Longer Than Anyone Else."*

Most of the time, Patrick can be found watching TV or sleeping. But that doesn't mean he can't move when he has to. Patrick can be downright speedy when he's frightened, or excited, or about to get ice cream!

*Patrick has been known to put on a tie for certain special events.*

*Starfish have hollow arms and breathe through their skin. They belong to a family known as echinoderms.*

## Sensitive soul

Though he's very sensitive, Patrick can also be brave. For example, he wasn't at all afraid to climb on the mysterious hooks that suddenly appeared in Bikini Bottom. Some might say he's brave because he doesn't understand the danger.

*Patrick's favorite hobbies include sleeping and lying dormant.*

## Undersea home

Ah, Home, Sweet Rock. Patrick loves his rock home because it's safe, warm, and easy to clean. He can lie in his bed, attach himself to the bottom of the rock, or use his whole house as a giant blanket. But the very best thing about Patrick's home is that it's only two houses away from SpongeBob's!

Patrick's usually a very sweet fellow, but he's capable of becoming very angry. When he thought SpongeBob had given him only a friendly handshake for Valentine's Day, Patrick became very upset, screaming "PATRICK NEEDS LOVE, TOO!" and "you broke my heart. Now I'm gonna break something of YOURS!"

# Squidward Tentacles

Squidward Tentacles is not the world's happiest octopus. He hates his job at the Krusty Krab and he wishes his noisy neighbors, SpongeBob and Patrick, would leave him alone. But life isn't all bad for Squidward—he does love playing his clarinet, painting self-portraits, and cooking gourmet food.

*Squidward's rubbery arms can throw snowballs faster than a pitching machine!*

## An educated octopus

Squidward *tries* to bring a little culture to Bikini Bottom. He offers art classes—but only SpongeBob shows up. He organizes a band—but no one else can play an instrument. He turns the Krusty Krab into a fancy restaurant—but with SpongeBob as the waiter, it doesn't last long.

## "Puh-lease tell me this isn't a joke."

*Most octopuses have eight limbs, but Squidward has only got six—four legs and two arms.*

## Head for home

Squidward's home is his refuge, his hideaway, his place where he rarely, if ever, invites SpongeBob to come over. In his studio, he makes statues and paintings of himself. In his kitchen he cooks gourmet meals for himself. And in his comfy bed, he can dream of a world with no SpongeBob.

Squidward enjoys modern dance, but he doesn't get many opportunities to practice. After a long day of working with SpongeBob, listening to SpongeBob, and living next to SpongeBob, he usually has a splitting headache. And when you've got a head like Squidward's, that's a big ache!

*Squidward's droopy nose is one of the biggest in Bikini Bottom.*

Squidward is smart, and his large head can be buffed to an impressive shine. His wide mouth is perfect for sighing, frowning, and telling SpongeBob to go away. Despite this, when Squidward lost his job, SpongeBob kindly offered him a place to stay.

*Squidward favors a dressy casual look and usually wears a collared T-shirt.*

## Octopus Facts

The smallest octopus grows to only 2 in (5 cm) long. But the biggest can grow up to 18 ft (5.5 m).

## Fun and games?

Squidward tries to resist SpongeBob and Patrick's silly games, but somehow he usually gets suckered into playing with them. The more he tries to avoid SpongeBob, the more he ends up lost in a kelp forest, deserted desert, or some other remote location with him!

# Bikini Bottom

The town of Bikini Bottom is a fascinating ocean community, full of quirky residents and interesting locations. Tourists flock to its Fry Cook Museum; the Bikini Bottom Zoo boasts the largest oyster held in captivity; and Goo Lagoon is home to Mussel Beach, THE hotspot for any undersea hunk.

Mrs. Puff's House

Jellyfish Fields

Sandy's Treedome

SpongeBob's Grandma's house

Squidward's house

Patrick's house

SpongeBob's house

Mr. Krabs' House

Mrs. Puff's
Boating School

Goo Lagoon

THE
KRUSTY
KRAB

The Krutsy Krab

Chum Bucket

Fry Cook
Museum

SHADY
SHOALS
REST HOME

Bikini
Bottom

Shady Shoals
Retirement Home

# SpongeBob's House

As most people know, SpongeBob SquarePants lives in a pineapple under the sea. But not just any pineapple—his is a comfortable home with a living room, a kitchen, a bathroom, a bedroom, and a well-stocked library! And it smells great!

## A place for everything

In his living room, SpongeBob watches TV and entertains guests. In the kitchen, he pours himself delicious bowls of Kelpo cereal. In the bathroom, he takes soothing bubble baths. In the library, he studies for his driving exam. And in the bedroom, he dreams of Krabby Patties and catching jellyfish.

*Chimney*

*Pineapple leaves hide rooftop terrace*

*Springboard for diving into bed*

*Treasure chest— contents unknown*

*SpongeBob's bed has three mattresses*

*Foghorn alarm clock*

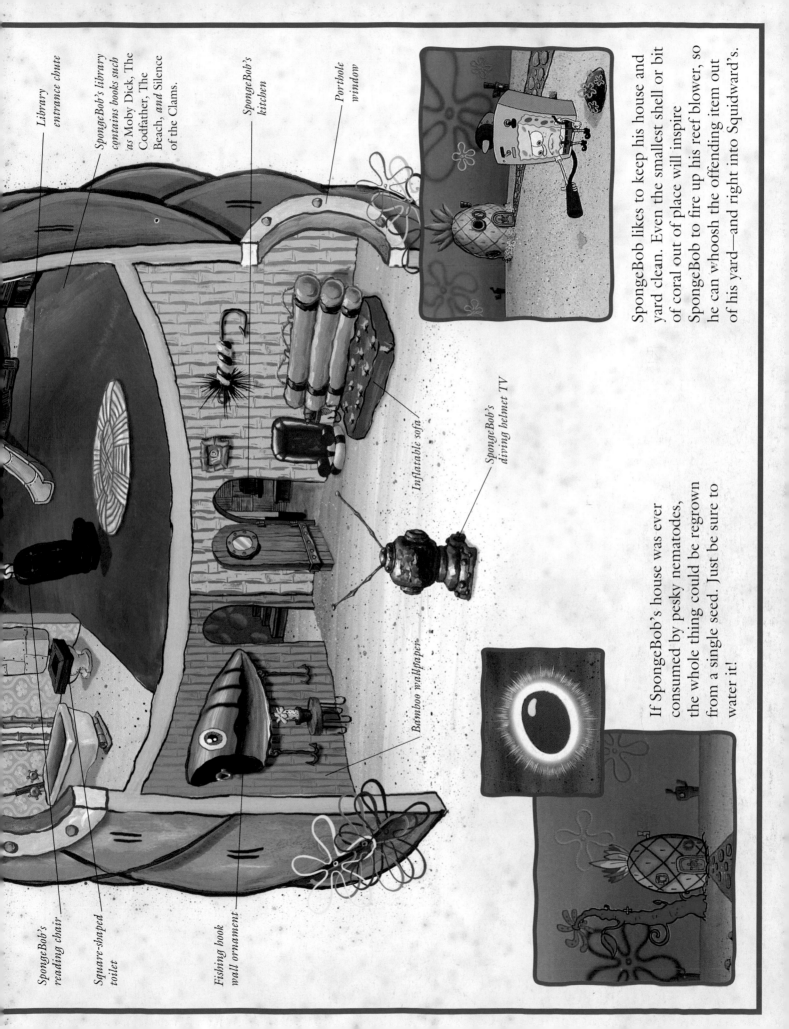

Library
entrance chute

SpongeBob's library
contains books such
as Moby Dick, The
Codfather, The
Beach, and Silence
of the Clams.

SpongeBob's
kitchen

Porthole
window

SpongeBob likes to keep his house and
yard clean. Even the smallest shell or bit
of coral out of place will inspire
SpongeBob to fire up his reef blower, so
he can whoosh the offending item out
of his yard—and right into Squidward's.

Inflatable sofa

SpongeBob's
diving helmet TV

Bamboo wallpaper

SpongeBob's
reading chair

Square-shaped
toilet

Fishing hook
wall ornament

If SpongeBob's house was ever
consumed by pesky nematodes,
the whole thing could be regrown
from a single seed. Just be sure to
water it!

# Eugene H. Krabs

**M**r. Krabs owns the Krusty Krab and runs it with a will of iron and a desire to earn as much money as possible. SpongeBob is his perfect employee—a hard worker who really doesn't care whether he gets paid or not.

## A crab's life

Mr. Krabs has led an interesting life. He was once the head chef on the *S.S. Diarrhea* before opening the Krusty Krab. He still keeps the first dollar he ever made in a frame. For a while, Mr. Krabs dated Mrs. Puff, the boat driving instructor.

*Mr. Krabs has amazing eyestalks— great for spotting missing money.*

Mr. Krabs' archenemy is Plankton, owner of the Chum Bucket. In one of his many attempts to steal the Krabby Patty recipe, Plankton built a robot version of Mr. Krabs to trick SpongeBob into revealing the secret formula. Luckily, Plankton's robot included a coin-operated self-destruct.

When it comes to money, Mr. Krabs is honest, but he hates to part with a single cent. Without money he's lost. As Mr. Krabs says, "If I don't make any money today, I'll surely break out in a rash."

*Mr. Krabs has two strong claws—great for grabbing money and never letting go.*

## Pearl

The only thing Mr. Krabs loves more than money is his teenaged daughter, Pearl. Though she loves her tight-fisted dad, he sometimes embarrasses her. Pearl is crazy about boys, clothes, makeup, and cheerleading. And she's pretty light on her flippers—for a whale!

## Anchor home

Mr. Krabs' home is shaped like an enormous anchor. On the walls of the living room hang a great many framed pictures. In Mr. Krabs' bedroom, there's a small hole in the floor that's always tripping him up.

*Mr. Krabs' legs are small but quick—great for running after money.*

# The Krusty Krab

The Krusty Krab is Bikini Bottom's finest fast-food dining establishment. With SpongeBob at the grill and Squidward at the cash register, satisfied customers eat Krabby Patties by the ton—and that means tons of money for its owner, Mr. Krabs!

## Shipshape seating

The big windows, kept sparkling clean by SpongeBob, let the customers see right into the spotless interior. Diners enjoy comfortable seating and convenient tables. Here they can eat and enjoy Mr. Krabs' famous hospitality—"No free napkins."

The beautiful exterior design of the Krusty Krab restaurant closely resembles a New England lobster trap. Maybe that's why Squidward feels trapped working there.

## Krabby Patty

Only Mr. Krabs and SpongeBob know the secret recipe that makes the Krabby Patty so delicious. If asked, SpongeBob responds, "The Krabby Patty formula is the sole property of the Krusty Krab and is only to be discussed in part or whole with its creator Mr. Krabs. Duplication of this formula is punishable by law. Restrictions apply, results may vary."

# Eager employees

SpongeBob and Squidward work as a team. SpongeBob chops the ingredients, fries the patties, puts the orders together, scrubs the kitchen, counts the sesame seeds, takes out the garbage, cleans the bathroom, mops the dining area, and scrapes gum off the bottoms of the tables. Squidward takes the orders.

The Krusty Krab kitchen is equipped for state-of-the-art frying. This is where Krabby Patties are made with love.

The Krusty Krab's cash register, set in a boat, supports the restaurant's nautical theme.

# Sandy Cheeks

Sandy Cheeks is Bikini Bottom's resident land creature. She's come all the way from Texas to live amongst the undersea life. Thanks to her air-filled Treedome, this squirrel is able to live comfortably at the bottom of the ocean. A lover of extreme sports, Sandy stays very active—unless she's hibernating.

## "Deep in my heart, I'll always be a Texas girl!"

## Squirrel fashion

When she's not inside her Treedome, Sandy wears a pressurized suit with air helmet that allows her to breathe underwater. The boots may look heavy, but they don't slow her down—she loves to burn carbs! Inside the Treedome, Sandy usually dons a stylish purple two-piece swimsuit.

## Texas

If you listen to Sandy talk, you might figure out that she's from the lone star state, Texas. Not only because of her accent or the colorful expressions she uses—"Ah'm hotter than a hickory-smoked sausage"—but because she's proud to tell people where she's from.

*This is Sandy's normal size. She becomes larger when she's hibernating.*

# Underwater respect

Sandy's come to love the creatures of the sea. The jellyfish impress her with their graceful movements. She's even learned to ride on their backs! The giant clams have amazing strength. And SpongeBob makes her laugh really hard.

Sandy's insignia is an acorn.

## Moon trip

Sandy's an adventurer, so she explores more places than just Bikini Bottom. In fact, she still keeps a rocket handy for occasional trips to the moon. Once, SpongeBob and Patrick launched Sandy's rocket without her. They ended up just looping around the moon and landing right back in Bikini Bottom, where they mistook everyone for disguised aliens!

Sandy loves to exercise. She runs inside her Treedome on an exercise wheel. Outside the Treedome, she surfs, snowboards, bike-rides, lifts weights, and loves to wrestle giant clams. With her best pal SpongeBob, she loves to practice karate, or as she says, "Ka-ra-tay."

# Sandy's Treedome

One of the most unusual locations in Bikini Bottom is Sandy's Treedome, a big bubble with an oak tree in the middle. To enter it, visitors have to pass through a special air lock. Inside, sea creatures wear helmets full of water so they don't dry out.

Inside her Treedome, Sandy has recreated the kind of home squirrels love, complete with grass, a picnic table, an exercise wheel, a bird bath, and an oak tree. The tree provides delicious acorns for her to eat!

Since her Treedome is full of air, Sandy doesn't have to wear her outdoor space suit, and can relax in an elegant swimsuit. She's proud of the air in her Treedome—"the driest, purest, most airiest air in the whole sea!"

## Home, sweet home

Sandy's Treedome is made of the strongest polyurethane, which she explains is a "fancy name for plastic." She had some of her friends from Houston help move all her stuff underwater and then she decorated the place to look just like her home back in Texas.

*Inside Sandy's oak tree there is a nice room for watching television.*

*Sandy's Treedome is the only place under the sea where you'll find grass growing.*

*The front door of the Treedome has a speaker so Sandy can greet her guests from inside.*

When he first visited Sandy's Treedome, SpongeBob was unfamiliar with the concept of air. He tried to convince himself that he could get along just fine without water, but soon he was drier than a Texas tumbleweed in the desert sun. A helmet full of Sandy's tasty iced tea soon brought him around.

## Exercise

Like many rodents, Sandy enjoys running on her exercise wheel. Dressed in her track suit, superfit Sandy could run for hours. If she hooked the wheel up to a generator, she could probably supply all of Bikini Bottom's electric power!

## Winter shutdown

When visiting Sandy one day, SpongeBob and Patrick were surprised to see the Treedome locked up and the inside full of white stuff! It was winter and Sandy was hibernating. Trouble occurred when the two got locked in and had to put up with freezing temperatures. They only managed to survive by making fur coats out of Sandy's hair.

# Mrs. Puff's Boating School

SpongeBob joyfully attends Mrs. Puff's Boating School—the finest (and only) boating school in Bikini Bottom. He's been there for quite some time trying, and failing, to get the one thing he's after most—his boating license.

## Driven to distraction

Mrs. Puff is a patient puffer fish, but even she has her limits. Thanks to SpongeBob's antics she's ended up in jail—more than once! Some days she considers moving to a new city and starting a new boating school with a new name. But then she thinks, "No, not again!"

*Mrs. Puff usually only puffs up to her full size when driven mad by SpongeBob!*

*Mrs. Puff can watch her students through her one-way chalkboard.*

**RULES OF THE ROAD**

Mrs. Puff's school is equipped with everything the student driver needs to get his or her license—a classroom, boatmobiles to practice driving, and an enclosed course for learning how to avoid obstacles. Of course, SpongeBob manages to make even an enclosed course dangerous.

*Mrs. Puff wears a blue and red driving teacher's uniform.*

# Classroom chaos

SpongeBob has problems inside the classroom, too. When Mrs. Puff asked him to write a 10-word sentence for extra credit, he completely froze. When a flounder named Flats decided to bully a fellow student, he chose SpongeBob. And when Patrick visited, he cost SpongeBob one of his Good Noodle stars.

## Puffer Fish Facts

There are about 90 species of puffer fish. Many are poisonous! They're also called swellfish or blowfish.

One of SpongeBob's proudest days at boating school came when it was his turn to be Hall Monitor. But he gave such a long acceptance speech that class was over before he got a chance to try on the uniform. So Mrs. Puff lent him the uniform for the night. When SpongeBob then took it upon himself to act as Hall Monitor for the whole town, Mrs. Puff knew she'd made an enormous mistake!

# Testing time

SpongeBob's taken (and failed) his boat license test 38 times. He always aces the oral part. He knows the answers by heart: the bow, the stern, starboard, port, skipper, deck, cabin, galley, keel, and 1924. But when it comes to the driving part, SpongeBob gets nervous and crashes, causing Mrs. Puff to, well, puff up!

# Jellyfishing

SpongeBob's favorite activity is the fine art of jellyfishing. The process is simple—catch the jellyfish, let it go, and repeat as many times as possible. SpongeBob is an expert! He also loves to get the jellyfish to squirt some jelly on a bun. Delicious!

## Underwater bees

Jellyfish are the bees of the underwater world and Bikini Bottom. They buzz around fields, live in hives, and sometimes sting. They also make a sweet, sticky, spreadable, edible substance—jelly. Jellyfish range widely in size, from a tiny little buzzer to a giant King Jellyfish.

*Jellyfish buzz as they fly through the water.*

*Jellyfish love to dance to music!*

Most of the jellyfish around Bikini Bottom live in Jellyfish Fields, a very popular jellyfishing destination. This is where SpongeBob goes when he wants to do a little jellyfishing on his five-minute lunch break. Jellyfish Fields is a wide-open, peaceful place where the jellyfish roam free.

JellyFish FIELDS

*Jellyfishing safety glasses*

*Jellyfish jelly tastes delicious on a Krabby Patty.*

# Safety first

Before you can go jellyfishing, you have to have the proper equipment: a net, jar, and safety glasses. The net is for catching the jellyfish, the jar is for storing jellyfish jelly, and the safety glasses are to make you feel safe!

# Born free!

Tired of his regular life, SpongeBob once went to live free and natural among the jellyfish. But after eating seaweed, crunching on coral, being bitten by poison sea urchins, getting stung by his brethren jellyfish, and being hunted by Patrick, SpongeBob happily returned to his home and friends.

## Jellyfish Facts

Jellyfish are almost 99 per cent water! Jellyfish have been around for hundreds of millions of years.

The most magnificent of all the jellyfish is *Cnydaria Rex*, the King Jellyfish. When he went jellyfishing with the Jellyfish Spotters, a group of elite jellyfishers, SpongeBob was able to tame the King Jellyfish with a bubble shaped like a pie, because as SpongeBob knows, "Everybody loves pie!"

# Sheldon J. Plankton

**P**lankton runs the Chum Bucket, the crummy fast-food restaurant across from the Krusty Krab. He longs to steal the recipe for Krabby Patties so everyone will come to his restaurant. Plankton may be small, but he's got big, evil ideas.

## "I went to college!"

## Patty prying

Plankton doesn't want the secret Krabby Patty formula just so his restaurant will succeed. He never gives up. In fact, he's been trying to steal the formula for over 25 years!

Plankton's antennae can detect a Krabby Patty cooking from miles away!

Plankton's analyst says he is one per cent evil, 99 per cent hot gas.

### Plankton Facts

The name "Plankton" includes all the tiny floating, non-swimming, animals in the ocean.

Plankton would love to devour a delicious Krabby Patty. He can hardly resist the enticing aroma and beautiful appearance of this wonder on a sesame-seed bun. But no matter how hard he tries, the faithful Krusty Krab crew stops Plankton from getting his tiny hands on a Krabby Patty every time.

# Cutting edge cookery

Plankton often relies on technology to carry out his evil schemes. He's invented mechanical legs for a Krabby Patty. He's attached a controller to SpongeBob's brain. And he's used robots several times—as fake customers, as a fake Mr. Krabs, and as a robo-chef to hold SpongeBob's brain. Nothing worked.

## Chum time

Since there are hardly any customers inside the Chum Bucket, Plankton doesn't need many employees—most of the time it's just him and Karen, his computer wife. But when he won SpongeBob from Mr. Krabs in a card game (after throwing the weekly games for 15 years), he gained the ultimate fry cook. SpongeBob succeeded in driving his new boss mad in less than a day!

*Plankton always enjoys an evil chuckle at the Krusty Krab's expense.*

Perhaps Plankton's smartest plan is holding on to his computer wife, Karen. She advises her husband on how to steal the secret Krabby Patty formula. But she also says his problem is "he never lets anyone in—Plankton the rock, Plankton the loner." Still, she loves him in her own cold way.

# Mermaidman & Barnacleboy

SpongeBob's favorite superheroes are Mermaidman and Barnacleboy. In their legendary crime-fighting days, the pair defeated the Sinister Slug, the Dirty Bubble, Man Ray, the Atomic Flounder, and the dreaded Jumbo Shrimp! Though they're a bit past their prime now, the two still jump into action whenever EVIL is afoot!

## Aquatic super powers

Mermaidman can summon the creatures of the deep. He can also throw water balls, and with his sidekick Barnacleboy, can dogpaddle in circles to form a whirlpool. When the "M" on his utility belt is pressed, it fires a "small ray" that shrinks milkshakes, people... even Bikini Bottom!

Nowadays, Mermaidman and Barnacleboy are retired, despite SpongeBob's best efforts to get them active again. They live at the Shady Shoals Rest Home, where Mermaidman enjoys the beds, the TV, and the meatloaf served in the cafeteria. He also likes prune ice cream with bran sprinkles.

*One of Barnacle Boy's super powers is his scorching sulfur vision.*

*Barnacle Boy is 68 and is beginning to look it.*

*Mermaidman has been fighting crime for over 65 years.*

By making life-size Krabby Patty mannequins of Mermaidman and Barnacleboy, SpongeBob won the conch signal—as seen on TV! This was the shell-shaped signaling device used to summon the dynamic duo when danger threatened. But SpongeBob used it to get help opening a jar of mayonnaise!

# Dressing up

SpongeBob and Patrick love watching the TV adventures of their favorite superheroes on Saturday morning while munching on bowls of Mermaidman and Barnacleboy Bran Cereal. But they REALLY love dressing up as Mermaidman and Barnacleboy and pretending to BE their superhero heroes!

Mermaidman's secret cave, the Mermalair, has a wall of superhero gadgetry, including the Cosmic Ray, the Aqua Glove, and the Orb of Confusion. These crime-fighting gadgets would be dangerous in the wrong hands—especially if those hands belong to SpongeBob and Patrick.

Superhero outfit— one size fits all!

Crime-fighting carpet slippers

Mermaidman's legs aren't as athletic as they used to be!

Mermaidman and Barnacleboy travel to their adventures in the Invisible Boatmobile. Barnacleboy thinks it was pretty stupid to make it invisible, since they always have trouble finding it. Luckily, they can use the Invisible Boatmobile Alarm.

# SpongeBob Sportspants!

SpongeBob is an energetic sponge. He's not one to just lie about all day. When he's not flipping Krabby Patties, he's likely to be playing a sport. It's all in good fun, unless Sandy's in charge, when it's all in good pain.

## Dressed for the part

SpongeBob enjoys the special clothing that goes with each sport. He also likes talking a good game, and making neat sound effects to accompany his efforts. But when it comes to the actual sport, things rarely go so smoothly!

*Even though his body absorbs sweat like a sponge, SpongeBob still likes to wear a sweat band.*

*SpongeBob can turn his body into a surfboard*

Sandy loves to skateboard, so SpongeBob is willing to give it a try. So far he's very good at slipping, scraping, crashing, and falling. And that's before he even steps on the skateboard!

It doesn't snow very often in Bikini Bottom, but when it does, you can be sure SpongeBob is right out in the white stuff— until he gets chilly and comes in for a nice cup of hot cocoa. Skiing WAS right up his alley—until he took a nasty spill and nearly injured himself seriously.

# Playing it their way

In Bikini Bottom, things are always a little different. When Patrick and SpongeBob play football, they follow their own rules. You might hear the two of them say something like, "You just lost three points! One! Two! Five! G–7!" "G–7? King me! King me! I lose!"

*SpongeBob owns "Anchor Arms"— big inflatable fake muscular arms.*

*SpongeBob's jogging pants*

# Karate

Karate is SpongeBob's absolute favorite sport. Wearing his protective gear, he loves to trade chops and kicks, even in the workplace, where he causes chaos. Once, Mr. Krabs threatened to fire him if he didn't give up karate. SpongeBob said, "I just can't help myself... you're gonna have to fire me." (Of course, Mr. Krabs didn't do that.)

Since he doesn't have his boat driver's license yet, SpongeBob is pretty much limited to walking, running, and biking. When you're biking across the bottom of the ocean you never get a flat tire, because instead of wheels, bikes are fitted with paddles.

# Taking a Break

After working hard and playing hard, a sponge needs to sit back and relax. SpongeBob brings just as much enthusiasm to relaxing as he does to everything else in life. And when it comes to relaxation, his best pal Patrick is in a class of his own.

## Catching rays

Since Bikini Bottom is an ocean town, people there love to lie on nice, comfortable lounge chairs and catch a few rays. How can you soak up the sun when you're underwater? Well... um... it's really quite... you just CAN, that's all!

*Although underwater, a sponge still needs to protect himself from the sun with some cool shades and a parasol.*

Of course, SpongeBob's favorite program is *The New Adventures of Mermaidman and Barnacleboy*, but when he's tired he'll watch other programs, too, including the Bikini Bottom news with its fish anchorman. Just don't ask him to watch... educational television!

When you're worn out after a tough day of flipping Krabby Patties, the only thing better than relaxing is relaxing with your best buddy. Unfortunately for next-door neighbor Squidward, SpongeBob and Patrick often involve him in their plans too.

DO NOT DISTURB

*Even when he's relaxing, SpongeBob wears his trademark shorts, shirt, and tie.*

# Happy hour

Life's one long holiday when you live in a beautiful ocean setting like Bikini Bottom. SpongeBob and Patrick love to sit back with an icy drink, relax, and enjoy the sounds of the sea and the surf.

# Gardening

SpongeBob finds it very relaxing to keep the yard around his pineapple neat and tidy. He spends hours tilling the soil and making sure that all of his plants are looked after with lots of tender, loving care. Some people would say that he's got green thumbs, which is odd, seeing as he's yellow.

*Patrick finds relaxing hard work, so he needs to go and lie down right afterwards.*

# Soak it up

At the end of a long day, SpongeBob loves to crawl into his tub and just soak it all in. And how does he feel when he's in a nice, hot bath? He feels swell!

# Pesky Pirates

When you live at the bottom of the ocean, you're sure to encounter the occasional sunken pirate ship. SpongeBob loves pirates—or at least he loves pretending to be one. He never misses an opportunity to dress up, shout "argh!," and try to board other boats!

## Treasure hunt

When they aren't getting dressed up as pirates, SpongeBob and friends like to play their pirate board game where they hunt for buried treasure using a toy map. Needless to say, with a game that involves hunting for money, Mr. Krabs soon became hooked.

Driven wild by the board game, Mr. Krabs took SpongeBob and Patrick on his pirate ship to look for the hidden treasure. And even though Mr. Krabs used the fake map from the game, they still found the buried loot! "Wow!" cried SpongeBob. "That game really IS based on a real treasure map!"

*SpongeBob once dressed up with two peg legs and called himself "Peggy the Pirate."*

*Squidward finds it difficult to get into the pirate frame of mind.*

*Mr. Krabs taught SpongeBob to say "argh," like a real pirate, not "okey-dokey."*

# Buried treasure

In SpongeBob's pineapple house there's an old wooden chest that looks very much like a pirate's chest full of treasure. What could be in it? Gold doubloons? Pirate's booty? Krabby Patties? According to Patchy the Pirate, even SpongeBob doesn't know because he lost the key!

# Painty the Pirate

Not to be confused with Patchy the Pirate, Painty is a pirate who's been trapped inside a picture frame. He has a patch over his left eye, a skull-and-crossbones hat, and a parrot on his left shoulder. This nautical nice guy is the painted pirate who leads us all in singing SpongeBob's theme tune.

*Patrick once dressed up with two eye patches and called himself "Blind Beard the Pirate."*

*When she's dressed as a pirate, Sandy's not afraid of anyone— not even the Flying Dutchman.*

# Perfect Pets

Like people in any other town, the residents of Bikini Bottom enjoy the company of their loyal pets. But instead of cats, dogs, and birds, Bikini Bottomites take care of snails, worms, and scallops. Or in Patrick's case, a rock.

## A feline snail

SpongeBob's pet is Gary the snail, an intelligent mollusk who provides his owner with hours of joy—and frustration, when he refuses to take a bath. Gary says "meow," purrs when he's happy, plays tag with SpongeBob, and enjoys the occasional bite of snail nip.

*SpongeBob's nicknames for Gary? The Gar Bear and Sweet Prince.*

*Gary usually meows like a cat, unless it's Opposite Day, when he barks like a dog.*

SpongeBob makes sure that Gary gets out and about. Besides walking him twice a day, he also likes to play fetch with Gary, no matter how long it takes. But SpongeBob carefully monitors Gary's exercise because he doesn't want his beloved pet getting too thin.

When SpongeBob went away to attend a jellyfishing convention, he made the mistake of trusting Squidward to take care of Gary. Thrilled to have three days without SpongeBob and Patrick, Squidward spent the whole weekend sunbathing, and forgot all about poor Gary. Luckily, all Gary needed to recover was a sip of water.

SpongeBob once adopted a jellyfish as a pet, even though Squidward warned him that it was a wild animal. SpongeBob and the jellyfish had a great time dancing together, until the jellyfish invited all its wild friends over to the pineapple and they trashed the place.

*Having your eyes on stalks is very handy for seeing around corners.*

GARY

# Wormy & Butterfly

Sandy has lots of pets, including Birdy, Snakey, and Wormy. When she left SpongeBob and Patrick in charge of them, the two friends especially loved playing with Wormy. Overnight, Wormy changed into a butterfly. When they looked through a glass at the butterfly's magnified face, they thought it was a horrible monster that had eaten Wormy!

## Pet from hell

Once, Gary left SpongeBob for Patrick, so SpongeBob got a new pet—a mean, hissing snail with one bushy eyebrow named Larry. Happily, Gary was only interested in the cookie in Patrick's pocket. When he'd eaten that he returned to SpongeBob and the two were reunited—Larry was sent packing.

# Goo Lagoon

Goo Lagoon is where everyone goes to swim, surf, sunbathe, play volleyball, and hang out. Goo Lagoon may be a stinky mud puddle, but to the residents of Bikini Bottom, it is a wonderful stinky mud puddle. What could be better than chilling out with your friends and letting the mud wash over you?

One guy you'll just about always find hanging out at Goo Lagoon is Larry the Lobster. When he isn't working as a lifeguard, he's playing volleyball, surfing, or lifting weights at Mussel Beach. Sometimes SpongeBob worries that Sandy might like Larry better than him. (We know she doesn't though.)

## Ready for anything

On his days off from the Krusty Krab, SpongeBob loves to hit the beach at Goo Lagoon. He always comes well-prepared, with plenty of equipment. That way, no matter what fun activity he's asked to join in, he can honestly reply, "I'M READY!"

## Beach life

To SpongeBob, the best part about going to the beach isn't splashing in the water or playing in the sand. It's being with his friends! Patrick loves being at Goo Lagoon with his pal. He also likes dozing in the sun and visiting the Snack Bar.

*Hamper packed with everything a sponge could need at the beach.*

# Pumping iron

Mussel Beach is the part of Goo Lagoon where all the big guys like Larry the Lobster go to lift weights. Sandy likes it, but SpongeBob prefers to work out in the privacy of his pineapple, where he can happily lift his bars with stuffed animals stuck on the ends.

Another guy who's constantly at Goo Lagoon is Scooter, the surfer dude fish. Scooter thinks the beach is totally "AWWWESOMMMME!" He also appreciates SpongeBob's humor. Scooter's hobbies include surfing, being buried in sand, and saying "awesome."

*With a body full of porous holes, SpongeBob struggles to get an even tan.*

One of the wildest things to do at Goo Lagoon is surf. The most famous surfer ever to hit the waves is Grubby Grouper. Larry the Lobster likes to lie down on his board. Sandy likes to do handstands. SpongeBob likes to surf, but he also likes to rip his pants.

*SpongeBob likes to match his Hawaiian shirt with an equally colorful pair of shorts to make the perfect beach outfit.*

# Lifeguard

SpongeBob's proudest day at Goo Lagoon came when Larry asked him to help lifeguard. As long as Larry was there, SpongeBob enjoyed himself, strutting around and blowing his whistle. But when Larry left SpongeBob in charge, he panicked and kept forcing everyone to get out of the water! SpongeBob forgot to tell Larry that he didn't know how to swim.

# Family Values

**P**eople in Bikini Bottom tend to have a lot of relatives. Plankton, for example, has so many he's able to form them into an army. SpongeBob and Patrick do not see their relatives every single day, so when they come for a visit, it's a very big deal.

## Doting sponges

SpongeBob's loving parents were thrilled when they thought their son would move back in with them after his house was eaten by nematodes. And when they thought he'd finally passed his driving exam, they ran right out and bought him a new boat with the license plate "IM-RDY." SpongeBob named it "Boaty."

*SpongeBob's grandma lives in a nice thatch-roofed cottage in Bikini Bottom.*

## Grandma

SpongeBob loves to visit his grandmother, since she bakes him cookies, reads him stories about magical sea leprechauns, and knits him sweaters with love in every stitch. When the guys at work tease him about her kissy-kissies, he's embarrassed, but secretly he likes kissy-kissies!

**Relative Facts**

Plankton has relatives named Billy-Bob, Billy-Jim, and Billy-Billy-Bo-Billy-Banana-Fanana-Fo-Filly.

*... and his hair style from his father.*

## Easily impressed

When Patrick's parents visited, Patrick was worried that they thought he was "dumber than a sack of diapers." SpongeBob volunteered to act incredibly stupid so Patrick would look smart. When Patrick's parents showed up, they were just impressed that he'd remembered to get dressed that day.

## Mama's pride

Mama Krabs looks quite a bit like her son, except that she wears big glasses and a purple dress. She's very proud of her son and his restaurant. She has a tendency to stub her toe painfully on rocks. But she never uses bad "sailor words."

Mama Krabs' home is right in Bikini Bottom. Like her son's house, it's shaped like an anchor, but it's pink instead of black, and is a little bit smaller than Mr. Krabs' house. Everything inside is neat and tidy—just like Mama Krabs.

# Bad Guys

Plankton isn't the only bad guy in Bikini Bottom. If there weren't any other bad guys, who would Mermaidman and Barnacleboy bring to justice? Although sometimes terrified by villains, SpongeBob can usually annoy them enough to leave him alone!

*The Flying Dutchman was forced to release SpongeBob when he became too annoying.*

## Pirate peril

Floating high above the sandy seabed, the ghostly Flying Dutchman is a particularly scary bad guy. If you're REALLY bad, he'll take you down to Davy Jones' locker for all eternity. Which is horrible, since Davy Jones works out a lot, and leaves his smelly socks in his locker.

*No self-respecting pirate would be without braids in his beard.*

SpongeBob and Patrick once served as the Flying Dutchman's crew. After they ruined all his attempts to scare people and scraped holes in his ship, he decided to eat them. But by stealing his dining sock, they forced him to grant them three wishes, so SpongeBob wished him into a vegetarian.

*The Flying Dutchman likes to wear his dining sock over his ghostly tail when he's about to munch on his kidnapped captives.*

## Villains galore

The evil Man Ray was frozen in tartar sauce at the Mermalair until SpongeBob and Patrick set him free. With the Dirty Bubble and Barnacleboy (who had turned to the darkside to earn some respect), he formed an alliance called E.V.I.L.— "Every Villain Is Lemons."

The Dirty Bubble likes to make others eat dirt and holds them captive inside his awesome bubble surface!

*The Flying Dutchman can shoot fire out of his nose.*

Despite his slippiness the Sinister Slug doesn't frighten Mermaidman and Barnacleboy—it takes more than some sticky slime to scare them!

Even though he's retired now, the Atomic Flounder is still perfectly capable of inflicting third degree burns, as Barnacleboy painfully learns.

The Jumbo Shrimp may not sound all that terrifying, but with four muscular arms, he can inflict plenty of damage!

*Even when he's asleep in his bunk, the Flying Dutchman wears his pirate uniform, ready to scare any unsuspecting passer-by.*

# Frankendoodle

When a magic pencil fell into SpongeBob's yard, he doodled a drawing of himself to play a prank on Squidward. However, the doodle came to life and proved evil. He beat up Squidward, stole the magic pencil, drew a deep pit for SpongeBob and Patrick to fall into, and worst of all, tried to erase SpongeBob!

# Party Time!

Spongebob loves a good party. His friends do, too, but they'd much rather laugh and dance than follow SpongeBob's detailed party plan. SpongeBob firmly believes that to achieve soiree success, it's crucial to stick to a firm schedule. After all, as he puts it, "Unsupervised partying can lead to disaster!"

## Entertaining etiquette

Patrick considers himself an expert on proper social behavior. Before SpongeBob has tea with Sandy, Patrick coaches him to act fancy by holding his pinkie up while he sips from his cup. When SpongeBob holds up his pinkie, Patrick approves: "Now that's fancy. They should call you SpongeBob FancyPants!"

When SpongeBob returned from trying to live in the wild, he was a sad sponge until he found his friends throwing him a surprise "Welcome Home" party! SpongeBob ate a Krabby Patty, and they all hugged—which was unfortunate, since SpongeBob had a bad case of itchy Poison Sea Urchins and passed it on to the others.

*When Patrick lists his favorite party activities, he often includes building a house of cards.*

# Food and drink

At one of his parties, SpongeBob baked a fish piñata and stuffed it with deviled eggs. He also followed a recipe from *Fun With Cream*, telling Gary to call an astronomer because the clotted cream was OUT OF THIS WORLD!

SpongeBob always makes his own delicious punch for his parties. Then he adds a special touch: a big chunk of ice carved to look like himself!

*At his parties, SpongeBob likes to read aloud from the newspaper comics.*

## Party Schedule

8:00–8:05 Guests arrive

8:05–8:15 Opening remarks and general discussion

8:15–8:27 Name tag distribution

8:27 Begin the qualifying round for cracker-eating-slash-tongue-twister contest

9:07 Running charades

9:38 Charity apple bob

9:57 Electric jitterbug dance marathon (ladies' choice)

10:09 Things start cooking as SpongeBob dips into his world-famous knock-knock joke vault!

**DK**

LONDON, NEW YORK, MUNICH,
MELBOURNE, AND DELHI

**Brand Manager** Rob Perry
**Project Editor** Catherine Saunders
**Publishing Manager** Simon Beecroft
**Category Publisher** Alex Allan
**DTP Designer** Lauren Egan
**Production** Rochelle Talary

First American Edition, 2005
Published in the United States by
DK Publishing, Inc.
375 Hudson Street
New York, New York 10014

This paperback edition printed for Scholastic Book Fairs in the
United States.

05 06 07 08 10 9 8 7 6 5 4 3 2 1

A catalog record for this book is available from
the Library of Congress.

ISBN-13 978-0-75662-081-3

ISBN-10 0-7566-2081-3

Color reproduction by Media Development and
Printing Ltd., UK
Printed and bound in China by
L. Rex Printing Co., Ltd.

Discover more at
www.dk.com